ORBIS CONNOISSEUR'S LIBRARY

EMPIRE STYLE
1804-1815

NIETTA APRÀ

ORBIS PUBLISHING LONDON

Contents

The photographs in this book were taken by G. Dagli Orti, with the exception of no. 2 which is from the Archivio Radaelli. The line drawings are by Aldo Ambrosini and Lino Bucciotti.

Translated from the Italian of Nietta Aprà

© Istituto Geografico De Agostini, Novara 1970
Translation © Orbis Publishing Limited, London 1972
Printed in Italy by IGDA, Novara
SBN 0 85613 126 1

The glittering Napoleonic era spanned in all only twenty years, including in its brief arc the periods of the Directorate, the Consulate, and the proclamation of the Empire (1804), before its eventual fall in 1815. It is however the eleven-year period of the Empire that gave its name to a style that was to characterize all the forms of art produced in France during those twenty years.

It is almost impossible to give precise dates to the evolution of an artistic phenomenon based on formulas and principles that interact and complement each other, but the dates of the Empire style can be established within certain limits – roughly from 1804 (the date of Napoleon's coronation as Emperor) to the end of his reign (1815) – largely because it was the Emperor himself who took up the task of dictating a style suggesting both greatness and severity, elements which are indeed its principal characteristics.

The *Directoire* style, the style that straddles the end of the eighteenth century and the beginning of the nineteenth, finds its origins in the passion for antiquity aroused by the famous excavations of Herculaneum and Pompeii, and from the writings of Winckelmann and others. This neoclassicism, as it has come to be called, was already widespread during the latter part of Louis XVI's reign; it constituted the moment of transition between the latter and the official Empire style, but it lacked the ostentation and pompousness of the Empire style proper, as it was to be in later years.

A love of everything recalling classical Greece and Rome became increasingly marked, and this one source of inspiration became the sole font of study and precise imitation.

The *Retour d'Egypte* style finds a place in this artistic evolution, originating as it does in the Napoleonic expedition to Egypt (May 1795–October 1799). Though it was not a true and individual style, it served to enrich the classical repertoire with a new exotic taste for decorative elements and themes drawn from Egyptian art, elements and themes imported and distributed principally by the designer, etcher and archaeologist Baron Dominique Vivant Denon (1745–1825), and made known to the French public by his work 'Voyage dans le Bas et Haut Egypte pendant les Campagnes du Général Bonaparte' (1802). This volume is rich with drawings and etchings of the most typical elements of ornament: sphinxes; caryatids; heads and bodies of mummified or stylized Egyptians with bare feet; palm leaves; tripods; rosettes; and so on. The author, archaeologist to the expedition, copied them from Egyptian temples, funeral columns and royal tombs, during the long journeys with Napoleon. All these motifs met with great favour in every branch of the decorative arts and persisted, albeit in a milder form, during the Imperial period.

The *Directoire* style, of which very few examples remain, maintained a certain elegance of line and proportion – not excessively heavy, its decorative vocabulary confined to few and somewhat stiff elements – while later on the Empire style proper turned decisively to the monumental, the noble, and imposingly severe.

Napoleon's contribution

Although providing the style with a name and title, Napoleon I did not contribute to its creation, nor was he guided in the choice by any aesthetic preference; his task was limited to the direction of an art style that was already established. This style he exploited as a basis for his grandiose schemes, creating a new and pompous regality that exalted his doings and his image. Napoleon's influence had social rather than artistic characteristics, and manifested itself mainly in the interest he took in the rebirth of industry and crafts, in the employment of the masses, and in the reorganization of the national industries, which he both patronized and helped with generous subsidies.

Nominated First Consul for life in 1802, Bonaparte immediately exercised his personal authority, having begun his frequent inspections of the major French industries in 1801. He visited the Gobelins manufacturers, and the cloth factories of Saint-Quentin, Bolbec, Elbeuf and Beauvais. In 1802 he visited the silk weavers of Lyons and explained to them the technological necessity of adopting mechanical looms, confronting the reluctant workmen with the new reality of the times: 'It is only with the adoption of mechanical procedures and a reduction in manual labour that French industry can cease to be inferior to the English.'

Once nominated Emperor, his contact with the working masses intensified and, between one campaign and another, Napoleon found the time to visit the drapers of Aix-en-

3

Provence, the factories of printed linen at Jouy, the *Manufacture* of Sèvres, and the mirror factories in the suburb of Saint-Antoine in Paris. 'All works of art and monuments are connected with politics', he said, and further: 'My aim is not to prevent this or that manufacturer from going bankrupt, since not even the coffers of the State would provide enough to help everyone; my concern is to prevent factories from closing their doors and leaving the working masses unemployed.'

All of the arts to which he turned his care and attention became, in his hands, instruments of a policy, the main aim of which was personal glorification.

The famous 'Mémorial de Sainte Hélène', edited by Emmanuel de Las Cases, offers us clear proof of Napoleon's lack of aesthetic taste when he recalls, in exile, his judgements and plans for the royal palace of Versailles (described by the official architects of the Empire as 'a deformed dwarf whose gigantic limbs, still more deformed, increase its ugliness'). 'Versailles', affirmed the Emperor, 'has always given me trouble. The Revolution would have rendered me a great service by destroying it, because nothing has been a greater waste or more useless than that immense building, and I have always condemned it. The Kings of France should have been satisfied with the residences of Fontainebleau, Saint-Cloud, Compiègne, the Tuileries and the others. In my gigantic projects for Paris I dreamed of using the palace of Versailles, in time, as a sort of suburb, a fascinating place to visit from the capital, and to adapt it to this function, I had worked out a singular plan, which had already been drawn up. I intended to eliminate all those statues of nymphs in the worst possible taste from the woods surrounding the palace [many of these statues were the work of leading artists of the time] . . . those Turcaret-type ornaments [a character symbolizing the nouveau-riche in a comedy by Lesage] and in their place I would have put panoramic stonework reconstructions of all the European capitals that we entered victoriously, with models of all the most famous battles which have given universal glory to our armies. There would also have been other monuments, as eternal testimonies to our triumphs and the glory of France. Situated at the gates of the capital of Europe, Versailles would have become the goal of visitors from every part of the world.' We can only be grateful that his dream was never realized.

Thus we can see that art, even in its lowest forms, was always placed at the service of Napoleon's essentially military genius, and of his desire to render his exploits and fame eternal.

The decisive and determining influence of Napoleon at a practical level is clear when one considers the abundant commissions given by him to various artists. All the official residences, for the most part stripped of their furnishings during the Revolution, were redecorated to their original splendour. The important people at Court, the new wealthy bourgeoisie, and the new-born aristocracy, could only follow his example, or rather his orders, and furnish their homes sumptuously according to the style dictated from above, perfected and created to the glory of the Empire and in the name of the Emperor. With the aim of recreating the pomp of previous courts, protocol obliged the ladies and gentlemen to dress more extravagantly and to maintain a luxurious standard of living.

Triumphs in architecture and art

Two architects, Charles Percier (1764–1838) and Pierre François Fontaine (1762–1853), were the two most important single figures in the field of Empire decoration and furnishing. Together Percier and Fontaine formed a partnership that lasted thirty-five years, and whose influence over every field of the decorative arts is comparable only to that exercised by Le Brun under Louis XIV. They followed the same course of studies in Paris, and later passed a number of years in Rome, dedicating themselves to the study of ancient monuments. On their return to France they were taken on by the furniture-makers, the Jacob brothers, with the assignment of designing furniture and plans for interior decoration. Later they were introduced to Napoleon by the painter David, and were appointed official architects to the First Consul and then the Emperor.

As architects their main duty was the renovation of the various royal residences – palaces, villas and castles – decorating their interiors in the new style. Their most important creations are the Arc de Triomphe of the Carrousel, the library of the castle of Compiègne, the small wing of the Louvre which connects with the Pavillon de Marsan, the throne room at Fontainebleau, and the decoration of the Galleries of Classical Antiquities at the Louvre. But their achievements go far beyond the role of architects and builders; in fact they became, in a short time, the true arbiters of taste in all branches of decorative art. They designed wall decorations, furniture, silver, *papiers-peints*, fabrics and china. The Empire style owes to them its unity of inspiration, and theirs is the merit of having known how to impose on the style of the new era the decisive orientation and homogeneity that are among its most evident qualities, even if these did degenerate at times to an excessively rigid monotony of architectonic realization and an exaggerated adherence to dogmatic schemes based on classical precepts.

Their aims were stated as a continuous attempt 'to imitate the classical in spirit, in principles, in general lines, which are valid for all time', and further, a determination never to 'try to find forms preferable to those left us by the ancient civilizations, whether in the field of creation or decoration'. In their important 'Recueil des Décorations Intérieures' (1812), we have the true handbook of the Empire style: a collection of an enormous number of prints, designs and plans, in which can be seen, side by side, copies of both Egyptian and Pompeian elements and motifs.

Painting, too, fulfilled the task of perpetuating the fame of Napoleonic triumphs; this field was dominated by the figure of Louis David (1748–1825). This superb painter, who had initially used his art to magnify the heroic and moral virtues of the ancients with the intention of glorifying the virtues of the Republic (as in, for example, 'The Oath of the Horatii', 'Brutus', 'The Rape of the Sabines'), dedicated himself with equal enthusiasm to the service of the new star who personified the ideal of the Empire. His powerful works became one of the most effective means of propaganda for the power of the new Caesar, and he signed them with pride *'Napoleonis francorum imperatoris primarius pictor'*, as one may see in the splendid portrait of Pius VII at the Louvre.

To David we owe some of the most celebrated historical compositions of the time: 'The Consecration of Napoleon' (1805–8) in the Louvre; 'Napoleon crossing the Alps' in Malmaison; 'The Distribution of the Eagles' (1810) in the Museum of Versailles.

But the true Empire painter, the foremost Napoleonic artist, is Antoine Jean Gros (1771–1835), favourite pupil of David, official artist to the Army, and eye-witness of some of the most glorious battles of the Imperial epoch. Gros owes his fame to the new spirit which informs his work, to the impressive immediacy of his paintings of battlefields in which the break with tradition is evident, where the tumultuous movement of masses, the strength of colour, observation of landscape and dramatic presentation of contrasts place him pictorially as forerunner of the romantic school. Gros was the first painter to depict the various aspects of war from a human viewpoint, portraying the less heroic side perhaps, but nearer the truth on the plane of historical reality. Among his finest compositions are: 'Napoleon on the Bridge at Arcole', 'The Battle of Abukir', 'The Plague Victims at Jaffa' (1808), 'The Battle-field of Eylau' (1808) at the Louvre, and 'The Battle of Wagram'.

Another artist who held a significant role at the Napoleonic court was Jean Baptiste Isabey (1767–1858), miniaturist and painter of full-scale canvases. From 1805 Isabey held the office of chief painter to the Empress Joséphine and to her successor, Marie-Louise, he held the office of chief decorator and 'director' of all the Imperial festivities. His porcelain snuff boxes decorated with miniatures depicting courtiers are famous, as are the Sèvres service and the celebrated 'Table of Austerlitz' or 'The Marshals', designed by Percier and decorated in bronze by Thomire.

Also worthy of mention are the painters Gérard (1770–1837), Girodet (1767–1824), Prud'hon (1758–1823), and the great Jean Auguste Dominique Ingres (1780–1867), another pupil of David, whose best works were done during the Napoleonic period.

Empire furniture

Just as the breeze of grace and airiness had swept away the heavy shapes of the Louis XIV style in the Regency period and later in that of Louis XV, creating lighter and more imaginative forms, so the appearance of the Empire, with its rigidly geometrical furniture, dark and massive austerity, and the uniformity of its bronze decorations, imposed a new style of severity on the whole field of furnishing, limiting any possibility of inventive abandon. All creation was subject to preconceived ideas and the overall impression tends to coldness and silence.

Dark and light mahogany replaced the infinite variety of precious woods previously used, with exotic names like *bois de rose* (rosewood), *bois de violette* (purplewood), *bois satiné* (satinwood), and so on. Veneers were widely used on every available surface of chests of drawers, beds, tables, no longer enlivened by enchanting coloured inlays in delicate shades; only the golden reflections of bronze decorations with motifs drawn from the mythological repertoire of classical antiquity outline the massive structures.

Mahogany, a wood which comes from the Antilles and Cuba, fine-grained, extremely durable, with many varieties of figure, flame, rippled or plum-pudding, was widely used for the furniture at Court; blond mahogany was rarely used. But after the Continental Blockade, the importing of exotic woods became more difficult and recourse was had to maple, root yew, and burr elm, known as *loupe d'orme*. There are also rare examples of painted wood furniture, usually either white with the highlights picked out in gold or else completely gilded, that were designed especially for the furnishing of official residences.

In Empire furniture all mouldings disappear; the doors are quite plain or soberly decorated with bronze sculptures outlining the geometric structure. Ornament usually takes the form of stylized sphinxes, lions' heads, or eagles, carved in wood or cast in gilt bronze and applied. Large or small cylindrical columns, usually placed at the angles in such a way as to leave the corners visible were fashionable. But the most typical decoration consists of bronzes gilded in matt or burnished gold or in an antique green finish. Such decoration in the Empire style was the work of artists like Thomire, Biennais, Odiot and Auguste, who created real masterpieces using this technique.

Dominant motifs

A dominant motif of all the ornament of the Imperial era was the famous capital letter N enclosed in a laurel wreath, which appeared on thrones, chairs, carpets and cloths, along with others such as Napoleonic bees, the eagle with wings displayed and stars.

The Empress Joséphine was very fond of the swan emblem, a motif that is to be found throughout the state rooms at Malmaison, and which became an ornamental element on chair arms, *appliques* or lamp brackets, carpets, and curtains. Birds, griffins, dolphins, and centaurs complete the lexicon of animal inspiration. Crowns or wreaths of laurel and rosettes were very common on materials and as keyhole surrounds. These wreaths were often supported by branches, stylized palm leaves and acanthus, by winged Victories, sphinxes with bare feet, and Egyptian figures. Lighter motifs underlined the structure of the smaller pieces of furniture, like the characteristic Greek key border, ovolos, beads, and designs in heart or clover shapes.

Countless bronze motifs are copied from classical art or taken from mythology: the most frequent are figures of winged Victories in the act of distributing crowns or wreaths; Fortune mounted on a globe; seahorses, battle trophies, swords, lyres, and various kinds of antique musical instruments.

Mirrors

The Imperial era also created certain typical pieces, from the *grand miroir* (great mirror, also known as a *psyché*), and the *table de toilette* (dressing table), to the *lavabo* (wash-basin), but much of the furniture was nothing more than an adaptation of pre-existing types with new formulas. The *psyché*, a large oval or rectangular mirror, framed in

*Above left: A grand miroir or psyché, a typical Empire piece.
Top right: A table de toilette (dressing table). Above right:
A ladies' small portable mirror*

mahogany supported by two columns, was always enriched
with gilt bronze plaques; branches of candelabra were
fixed to the supports, one on each side. Two legs in the form
of lions' paws or Egyptian figures supported the mirror.
Among the finest and most sumptuous examples, the
psyché made by Jacob to a design by Percier, which is
conserved at Compiègne, is worthy of mention. Simpler,
and corresponding to the feminine taste of the time, was
the *petit miroir portable*, a minute mirror framed in a heart
or shield shaped frame, attached on two pivots to side
supports with a drawer for toilet articles in the base. It
was so small that it was conveniently portable. One of the
finest examples of this type of mirror small enough to
balance on the knees is conserved in the bedroom of
Joséphine Bonaparte at Malmaison.

Ladies' furniture

Another creation of the Empire style was the *table de
toilette*, the most important feature of the elegant lady's
room. It was usually rectangular in shape, with a white
marble top, resting on legs in the form of an X or of
classical lyre shape, always superbly finished with bronze
ornamentation, the oval or rectangular mirror, with
bevelled edges, rising from the marble table and with
bronze supports incorporating candelabra. A superb
example, in flowering elm, made by Félix Rémond, can be
seen at Malmaison in the bathroom of the Empress
Joséphine; a second example, no less rich, is conserved in
Paris at the Musée des Arts Décoratifs. The *lavabo*, widely
found in the Imperial epoch, consisted of a porcelain base,
often from the factory of Sèvres, supported on three
wooden legs decorated in gilt bronze, or on an iron tripod
known as an *athénienne*, also used earlier for a certain type
of *bonheur-du-jour*. The basin was quite wide and deep –

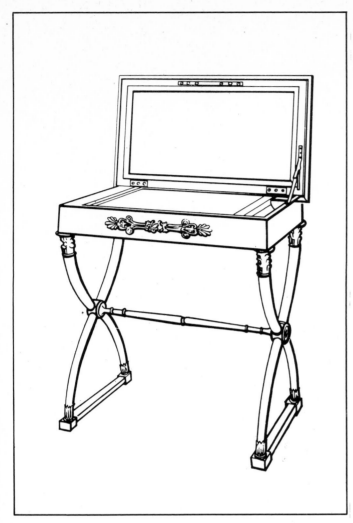

although its proportions may strike us as modest – and seems to have sufficed the limited demands of hygiene made on it by the elegant and perfumed Imperial ladies. Also known as the *saut-de-lit*, or 'jump-out-of-bed', the wash-basin formed part of the *petits meubles* or smaller pieces of furniture, and was completed by a stand for the water jug. Among the most sumptuous examples the two conserved in the suites at Malmaison and a third at Fontainebleau are worth recording.

Consoles

The *consoles* represent an essential piece of furniture of the Imperial period: they are for show, furnishing state rooms or ante-rooms or serving as side-tables. Having lost the graceful gilt finish typical of the preceding centuries, the *console* continued to be widely used, although it acquired a more solid appearance. The rare marble top rested on a mahogany frame ornamented with the familiar cast bronze motifs – rosettes, Greek key borders and mythological scenes – it was supported against the wall with simple legs but at the front and sides were ponderous legs in the form of stylized caryatids, columns adorned with bronzes, chimeras, sphinxes, the whole resting on a simple mahogany plinth, decorated in its turn with carved motifs. The semicircular *console* at Malmaison, the work of Jacob Desmalter, is a beautiful example, supported by two bronze sphinxes.

Tables

Tables were generally circular, occasionally polygonal or rectangular, their tops of mahogany, marble, porphyry and in some cases of glass or porcelain, particularly in the case

Left: Table de toilette, with its mirror inside a closing lid.
Below: Two guéridons – one with winged Victories, the other with heads, stars and swans

of small tables, supported by three or four legs, or a central column. Of the few remaining examples of rectangular tables, that of Jacob Desmalter at the Grand Trianon at Versailles is a real masterpiece. Table legs differed widely, from being pyramid-shaped to the triangular or circular, with motifs of griffins or lions' feet. A typical feature of the table was the reinforcing stretcher, which also served as a foot-rest. Sometimes an antique vase was placed at the centre of the base, or perhaps a sculpture, an incense burner, or a cup.

There was quite a variety among the small tables, each with characteristics of its own, with different names and well-defined uses, like the *guéridons*, which could be circular or octagonal, with a top and base of equal size, joined by small columns, the base carrying a decorative two-handled vase or carved basket of flowers.

The *tables à fleurs* or flower tables, popular during the Directorate, came back into fashion with the Empire; usually circular, the top was supported by columns resting on a base. The top was encircled by a painted metal gallery which served as a flower container. If one thinks of the many designs by Percier, one can only conclude that this type of table was immensely popular in the furnishing of Imperial rooms.

The *bouillotte* table, a circular table of smaller proportions inherited from the Louis XVI period, is linked, like the lamp of the same name, with a card game similar to the Italian *briscola*, then very fashionable. The *bouillotte* table had a marble top surrounded by a metal frieze provided with drawers.

Left: Classical caryatids on an Empire console. Below: Drawings of two other Empire tables give an indication of the great variety of table legs produced at this time

The night tables (known as *somnos*) were shaped like columns, or votive altars, heavy, massive, and laden with bronze ornaments. They were placed one on each side of the bed.

Tall pedestals were very popular as stands for statues, lamps, precious pieces of porcelain and sculpture. Shaped in pyramid or pillar form they were always decorated with valuable gilt bronze ornaments.

Chests and cupboards

Of the smaller pieces of furniture there remain the useful *vide-poches* (pocket emptiers), and the important *serre-papiers* (paper-holders) of which a fine example exists in Napoleon's study at Malmaison (illustrated on page 48). The large pieces of furniture (chests of drawers, *secrétaires*, desks, cupboards) no longer had the imaginative variations of the preceding centuries but, rigid in form, followed the austere lines fashionable at the time. The decorative schemes are the only real point of originality to be found in these large pieces.

The *bas-d'armoire*, a sideboard with a cupboard below, was more popular than the chest of drawers. With its rectangular box shape and two or three doors opening on to a series of drawers, it offered an opportunity for original decoration, which helped to break up the severe lines of this type of piece.

Another piece of furniture that was revived rather than invented during this period was the *cabinet*, which derives from an eighteenth-century formula. This was a small cupboard with a lid, doors and drawers, and was used to furnish bedrooms or libraries.

The *armoire à livres* of the eighteenth century, graceful and elegant in shape, gave way to a large piece of furniture resting against the wall. This latter had several rows of shelves supported by columns with ornamental motifs in bronze sculpture; the lower part, closed by two doors, was separated from the upper by a flat plane. Used as bookshelves, these huge pieces of furniture almost completely covered the walls against which they were placed.

Desks

There were four different models of desks during the Empire period: the simple desk or *bureau plat* of the past century, which rested on four legs connected by a stretcher; the *bureau à cylindre* of which Percier designed some examples, but which tended to die out; the *bureau ministre* in two sections which had drawers that were symmetrically placed and symmetrical bronze ornament, and, finally, the mechanical desk created by Jacob Desmalter for the Emperor's study at the Tuileries, with a sliding lid that covered the whole surface but did not disturb the precious papers. At Fontainebleau there are several examples of this type of desk which appears to have been greatly appreciated by the Emperor. The one used by Joséphine at Malmaison was made by the Jacob brothers to a design by Percier and Fontaine (about 1800), constructed in the form of a triumphal arch enriched on the sides by a finely modelled gilt mount of winged griffins; at the four corners figures of winged Victories held up the heavy top.

The *bonheur-du-jour*, a type of small, feminine *secrétaire*, continued to flourish under the Empire. More rigid in

Two of the many different styles of chair produced in the Empire period. In general Empire chairs were massive and constructed in heavy woods such as mahogany

form, it nonetheless had a pleasant appearance. It was formed by a small table on which rested a small cupboard full of tiny drawers; it bore the usual decoration in gilt bronze, the back legs were plain, while the front were embellished with decorative gilt feet. A splendid example, the work of Lemarchand, is in the Musée des Arts Décoratifs in Paris.

Beds

Beds may be divided into two types: the *lit en bateau* (boat bed), and the bed with a straight head and foot rest. The former, which is the most common, is the typical

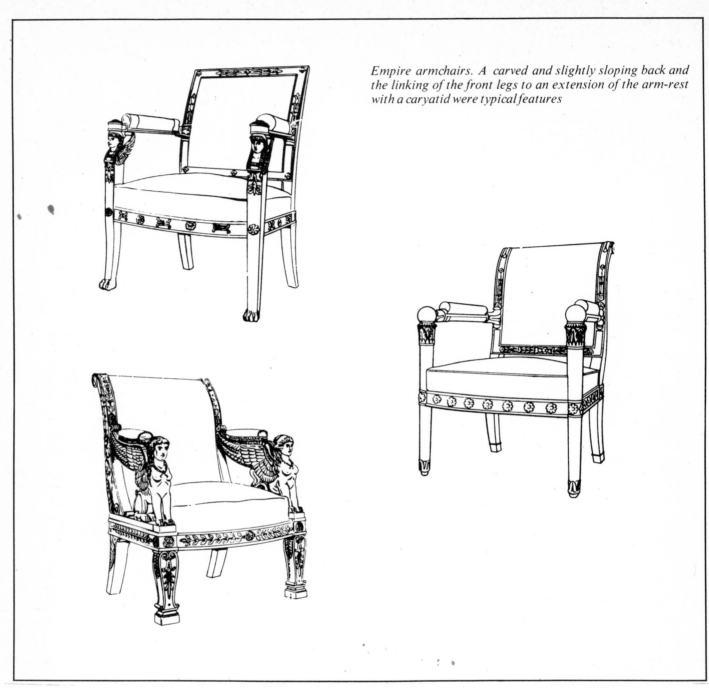

Empire armchairs. A carved and slightly sloping back and the linking of the front legs to an extension of the arm-rest with a caryatid were typical features

Empire style bed. Both the bed-head and foot were of equal height, and either straight or curved outwards in such a way as to suggest a ship – hence the name *lit en bateau*. The *lit en nacelle* derived from the former, its head and external edge forming a continuous curve, resting on a rectangular base. Bronze ornament featuring diverse motifs was distributed along the outer edge and bed-head supports. The beds with straight ends, a strict derivation from the Louis XVI model, took on new characteristics: the end supports were enriched by pillars topped with antique vases, sphinx heads and caryatids. It was typical of these beds that the supports that leant on the wall side were higher than those on the outside, and ended in rich curtains and a canopy. This canopy, suspended from high up on the wall, was gathered at the head to form a sort of sleeve, often surmounted by a gilt frieze.

Chairs

Chairs of the Empire period are numerous and show a surprising variety of detail. In general they were massive, and constructed in heavy wood. The armchairs commonly had a curved and slightly sloping back, while the chairs had a straight back, perpendicular to the seat, the back legs sabre shaped, the front finishing in an animal paw or column. One of the characteristics of the Empire armchair was that the front legs were linked to an extension of the arm-rest by a sculptured figure of a caryatid, or a swan with spread wings. The *en gondole* armchair is perhaps the most graceful of all the various forms produced in France during this whole period.

Another typical chair, the *fauteuil d'officier*, should be mentioned also. This was specially designed so that the soldiers could sit down without the bother of removing their sabres.

Tabourets or stools with X legs were very common, the X representing crossed swords. Protocol demanded that even during family reunions, only the Emperor, Madame Mère and the Empress should sit in armchairs; the others had to be satisfied with *tabourets*. There was also the *méridienne*, a type of small sofa, the two ends of which were of different height, with the back correspondingly higher at one end than the other; another form of *méridienne*, the pannier, had both sides equal, becoming a normal sofa for two like the one in the portrait of Madame Récamier painted by David.

The *chaise longue*, also known as *lit de repos*, is quite rare in the furniture of this period. It was often divided into two halves, similar to the old type called *duchesse brisée*.

Chairs, armchairs, *canapés* and stools were generally made of mahogany. The show pieces, in official residences, were usually completely painted white with a gold thread, or coloured completely in light grey or pale green. The bronze ornaments of mahogany furniture are to be found in the usual motifs on the arms, legs and framing of the back. They were luxuriously covered and upholstered in silk, fine velvet or tapestry, with bewitching tints of green, yellow and crimson, which harmonized softly with the curtains, firescreens and walls.

Tapestries, fine carpets and silks

Despite Napoleon's protection, frequent visits of encouragement and generous subsidies, the products of the *Manufacture* of the Gobelins did not succeed in regaining the quality and prestige they had achieved in the preceding centuries.

Guillamon, appointed Director, carried out Napoleon's orders for tapestry reproductions of pictures and sketches by living artists, representing the historic moments of his glorious reign, to furnish the various residences of the court with the magnificence worthy of the Emperor of France. Tapestries like 'Napoleon crossing the Alps' by David, 'The Plague Victims of Jaffa' by Gros, 'Napoleon receiving the Keys of the City of Vienna' by Girodet, 'The Death of Desaix' by Regnault, were typical. There were also enormous orders for door curtains with allegorical figures, usually in classical style, and tapestry for covering chairs, stools, armchairs, divans in which the motifs dear to the Emperor prevailed.

The manufacturers of Beauvais also worked for the Court: the director was the artist Jean-Baptiste Huet, who could be said to excel neither in technical gifts nor in composition, and who on the whole merely repeated the decorative motifs of the Empire style.

In the workshops of Aubusson, Percier and Fontaine set out motifs and models drawn from the most severe classic formulas and provided designs for the *moquettes* then in fashion which were produced for the Emperor and his nobles on the premises of the Savonnerie factory.

A crisis had struck the ancient and famous carpet works of Savonnerie, lasting from 1789–99, roughly the years of the Directorate, when it produced simple carpets with poor designs and bad colours. The crisis was resolved by Napoleon and the new nobility, through numerous and continuous orders for the adornment of both Imperial and private houses. Among the many designers working at Savonnerie, the decorator La Hamayade de Saint-Ange was the best. Appointed designer to the Mobilier Impérial in 1802, we owe to him the best of the carpet designs. The motifs most frequently used are the large central rose design enclosing the Imperial N, an eagle crowned, and the swan, which, as we have said, was a symbol dear to the Empress Joséphine, while the borders were enriched by sequences of palm leaves, stars and other classical-type motifs. Soft beige tints formed a background to the compositions realized in brilliant colours, thereby creating a combination of sober elegance and decorative restraint which clearly distinguish them from other contemporary makes of carpet.

In the billiard saloon at Malmaison, there is perhaps the only Empire-style carpet still intact today (few examples survived the drastic treatment of the newly established monarchy, intent on destroying and replacing every trace of the Napoleonic period). It covers almost the whole floor, and is decorated with the well-known Napoleonic emblems: N, bees, stars, thunderbolts, and so on.

Almost destroyed, or at any rate inactive during the Revolution, the silk factories at Lyons attempted a laborious recovery during the Directorate and the Consulate until they finally regained full activity in the Imperial period; this recovery was entirely due to the particular interest Napoleon took in them with the hope of restoring to them their original place as the first in Europe.

Important orders for precious silks were issued by the Imperial house for the redecoration of salons in official residences, palaces and castles; the Imperial example rendered it more or less obligatory for the members of government and Court to furnish and decorate their homes more extravagantly. The walls of large salons, rooms and boudoirs were covered in miles of curtaining and silk panels, not to mention door curtains, bed covers, upholstery for divans, chairs and armchairs.

The protocol of the new Court demanded, as we have seen, the use of extremely rich costume – both male and female – with the double aim of helping the national industries 'to give employment to those without work in the poor zones of Paris' and to revive the splendour of past Courts. In his famous 'Journal des Dames et des Modes' the abbot La Mésangère described the rich styles of dress requiring velvets, silks, embroidery, ribbon and lace over the period from 1797–1832.

A vast quantity of silk fabrics was produced at Lyons to satisfy the demands of Imperial fashion; the *taffetas cannetés* were very popular, as were the *gros de Tours*, brocades with gold thread; velvet too was much in demand, in splendid colours of dark green, deep purple, deep blue and crimson; also popular were the damasks on a background of blue or tobacco colour, and heavy satins in green, rose, or pale violet with decorations in old gold.

The most common design was *en camaieu*, in chiaroscuro with motifs inspired by antiquity, stylized leaves, laurel wreaths and oak.

The usual motifs of Imperial decoration, like the bees, swans, stars, eagles, palm leaves, and laurel wreaths, were to be seen everywhere, dominated of course by the Napoleonic N.

Prints on textiles

Napoleon followed with equal interest the activities of the factories of printed cloth and linen at Jouy. These materials, created by the German dyer Oberkampf in 1760, during the last years of Louis XV's reign, enjoyed a deservedly long period of popularity. About the year 1798 the discovery of new processes and techniques permitted the prints a wider range of colours, and pastoral scenes, such as the fables of La Fontaine, were produced, unfolding on a soft background of ivory colour, lilac or sand, to the designs of Jean-Baptiste Huet.

With the coming of the Empire and Napoleon's generous protection, the beautiful printed linens or canvases included motifs of sphinxes, triumphal arches, mythological scenes and battles – in short, the whole repertoire of the epoch.

Rivals and competitors with Jouy were the factories of Nantes, Orange, Rouen and many others to such an extent that at the Exhibition of 1806, about a hundred and fifty manufacturers presented their various products.

It is important to remember that a great part of the French textile industry's good fortune is owed to the invention of the mechanical loom by Joseph-Marie Jacquard (1752–1834), whose first model was put on show at the Industrial Exhibition of 1801.

Empire porcelain from Sèvres

Under the Empire, the production of porcelain at Sèvres recovered its former activity if not the splendour enjoyed during the Ancien Régime. Having hardly survived the revolutionary cataclysm, Sèvres achieved a limited production under the Directorate. Porcelain and earthenware reflected the symbols of the time, adopting motifs from the Revolution: red republican caps, tricolour cockades, representations of the goddess Reason, trees of liberty and so forth, while busts of Robespierre, Danton and Marat were modelled in biscuit.

Once he had become First Consul, Napoleon went to work to restore the celebrated factory to its original dignity, visiting it between one campaign and another and encouraging its revival with the help of large subsidies.

In 1800 Napoleon appointed Alexandre Brongniart (1770–1847) Director of the Sèvres *Manufacture*, and he rapidly reorganised the concern. In order to obtain a greater, faster and cheaper method of production, the new Director abandoned soft paste in favour of the exclusive use of hard paste, thereby sacrificing the capricious grace of form, delicate shapes and subtle modelling that could be achieved with soft paste, and which had characterized the masterpieces of fantasy, elegance and delicacy that had made Sèvres ware world famous in the eighteenth century.

Shapes under the Empire assumed different and simpler lines: the cups lost their lightness of form to become rigidly cylindrical; the graceful jugs turned into amphoras and heavy wine cups of classical inspiration; sugar bowls became miniature tripods. Painted decoration followed the Imperial formulas: classical ruins, recent historical events, glories of the Napoleonic armies, portraits of the Emperor, of Joséphine and of Marie-Louise, mythological figures, stars, bees and Roman swords – all these ornament the wide plate rims, the bottoms of sugar bowls and the brims of the large amphoras. The Egyptian inspiration also persisted in saucers covered with hieroglyphics and in cups with palm leaves and pyramids. Gold was widely used on the inside surfaces of cups and vases, matched with deep reds, dark blue and black.

Napoleon ordered various types of china service from Sèvres, with pictures of the Imperial residences; at Malmaison one may still find magnificent plates reproducing the waterfalls of Saint-Cloud, Malmaison, the hunt at Boutard; a large wine cup has images of the Emperor in front of the castle of Potsdam. The edges of the plates and rims of vases gleam with gold on a background of 'Corsican green', Napoleon's favourite colour. Worth recalling, too, are the Austerlitz vase at Malmaison, in the form of a large amphora coloured red on black, with the portrait of Napoleon in the robes of a Roman emperor standing majestically in a chariot; and, another example of the propagandist function assigned to art by the Emperor, the 'Table of the Marshals' or 'Table of Austerlitz', an elaborate composition celebrating the famous battle and the marshals who contributed to the great victory. In the centre of the circular top is a portrait of Napoleon in grand Court costume; he symbolizes the sun from which thirteen rays terminate in medallions depicting miniatures of the thirteen marshals; allegorical figures in biscuit comprise the central column support which rests on a gilt bronze base. This spectacular piece was made at Sèvres, the bronzes being by Thomire, the miniatures by Isabey and the design by Percier.

Besides the factory of Sèvres, one should also recall that of Honoré Dagoty, patronized by Joséphine, who permitted him to use her name for his wares. Dagoty made the cup presented to Marie-Louise by Napoleon at Parma, a magnificent piece in porcelain and gold, with the emblem of the Empress Marie-Louise and various allegories of Love.

Opaline

The great popularity enjoyed by opaline during the Empire is worth mentioning. This material was produced in the preceding century with glass called 'milk white'; in the Napoleonic period, however, opaline was made of the purest transparent crystal, and was among the finest and rarest of its kind. The pieces are designed with extreme delicacy and are soft and ephemeral in tone, including white with orange reflections, rose, yellow, pale blue and, most precious of all, glowing with lilac which has the splendour of pearl and was known as 'pigeon's throat'. The forms are, as usual, based on classical inspiration.

Metalworkers and their art

The art of working in metals occupies a place of honour in the Napoleonic period: gold, silver, bronze, and vermeil (silver gilt). The artist Henri Auguste (1759–1816), son of a goldsmith working under Louis XVI, distinguished himself in such work, as did Pierre-Philippe Thomire (1751–1843), Jean-Baptiste Claude-Odiot (1763–1850), and Martin-Guillaume Biennais (1764–1843).

The greatest, however, was Philippe Thomire, whose outstanding personality dominated the first part of the Empire. After early studies with Pajou and Houdon, the artist became a pupil of the great Gouthière who formed his preference for gilding *à mat* (matt gold). Under the Ancien Régime Thomire created admirable, finely moulded bronzes for one of the beautiful desks ordered by Louis XVI from the furniture-maker Bennemann; active at Sèvres during the Consulate period, he decorated the famous vases in porcelain and biscuit, modelled by Boizot, with splendid garlands in moulded gilt bronze. Shortly afterwards he was appointed titular metalworker of the Imperial *Garde Meubles*. He created his most famous pieces for Napoleon, whose high esteem he enjoyed, and by 1808 his *atelier* contained more than eight hundred workers engaged in satisfying the numerous commissions of the Court. Among his major works, the chiselled frieze depicting the nuptial procession applied to a porcelain vase offered by the Sèvres factory to Napoleon on the occasion of his second marriage, to Marie-Louise of Austria, should be mentioned.

Other products of Thomire's fine ware include the bas-relief in silver gilt which enriched the cradle of the King of Rome (now in the Kunsthistorisches Museum, Vienna) depicting symbolically the Seine and Tiber, with an eagle poised for flight; the winged Victory supports a laurel wreath from which the drapes of the cradle are suspended, and the cradle itself rests on fine cornucopias. Thomire also created the splendid *psyché* mirror and *toilette* table in silver gilt adorned with lapis lazuli, given by the city of Paris to the Empress Marie-Louise on her wedding day; sadly, this splendid piece was melted down on the orders of the Empress when she became Duchess of Parma. The only idea that we have of what it looked like comes from the original designs of Thomire and Odiot, and the water-colour sketches of Prud'hon, who devised the original composition.

Thomire also created the gilt bronze parts of the already mentioned 'Table of Austerlitz', and almost certainly participated in the creation of the splendid *serre-bijoux* (jewel chest) of Marie-Louise. The Stibbert Museum in Florence houses Thomire's great table in malachite, ornate with sculpted figures of Zephyr, the god of winds. Thomire was also among the greatest makers of bronze mounts for furniture, and also one of Jacob Desmalter's most assiduous collaborators.

Henri Auguste (1759–1816), son of Robert Joseph, goldsmith to Louis XVI, was appointed master goldsmith in 1785. When the Empire began he was forty-five years old, and one may say that the major part of his production is connected with the Ancien Régime since he continued to work in the spirit of the eighteenth century, even under the Empire rule. He was among the first to make use of the technique of fusion and 'cold mounting'. The city of Paris commissioned him to work on a monumental table service in *vermeil* as a present for the Imperial couple on their coronation (1804). The original work was to be of 590 pieces, requiring more than 12 hundredweight of silver, but it was never finished by Auguste, who went into exile in 1806, after going bankrupt. Apart from the 22 pieces preserved in the dining room at Malmaison, all the others were melted down during the brief reign of Charles X.

Among the remaining examples, the most outstanding are the elegant and decorative vessels (*nefs*) destined for the Emperor and the Empress. It had been a tradition from medieval times for the city of Paris to present such a vessel to the new monarch for his personal use, to contain his table accessories and so avoid the danger of poisoning. Napoleon's example, in the form of a sailing vessel, is supported by two female figures symbolizing the Seine and the Marne, resting on a high base adorned with a radiant letter N. The prow is surmounted by the figure of Victory, while seated in the poop are the symbols of Justice and Prudence. The sides of the vessel bear bas-reliefs representing the 12 municipalities of Paris, the coronation of the sovereigns and the presentation of the gift on the part of the prefect and councillors of the city.

The vessel of the Empress, similar in form to the Emperor's, is different in its allegorical decoration: here there are the three Graces and Beneficence. On the base of both pieces this inscription is to be found: 'Henri Auguste, 1st Year of Napoleon's reign'.

Jean-Baptiste Odiot (1763–1850), who was descended from a family of goldsmiths, was not only a metal chaser but a designer as well. The Musée des Arts Décoratifs in Paris possesses a service made by him in silvered bronze in which the form and decoration are purely classical in style, and are for the most part taken from designs by Percier and Fontaine. Taking advantage of the bankruptcy of Auguste the goldsmith, Odiot got hold of his designs and models to help him to complete the service in *vermeil* presented to Napoleon on his coronation by the city of Paris. Odiot was one of the bronze workers who contributed to the decorations on the cradle for the King of Rome and to those on the *psyché* mirror and *toilette* table presented to Marie-Louise by the city of Paris.

Martin-Guillaume Biennais (1764–1843) was a goldsmith, jeweller, furniture-maker and arms dealer, a rival in this latter activity of Nicolas Boutet, designer of most of the parade swords of Napoleon. Biennais began his artistic career as a furniture-maker and, in 1800, settled in Paris where he opened a shop under the sign of the 'Singe Violet' (mauve monkey). From this first period dates a *serre-papiers*, a small piece of furniture intended to keep manuscripts and journals in order, today in the library of Malmaison. Also at Malmaison in the Empress's rooms there is a tiny writing desk in thuya wood, inlaid with silver, on which one may read the signature and mark: 'Biennais, goldsmith to their Imperial Majesties and Court and to His Majesty the King of Holland and Westphalia, Paris, Singe Violet, Rue Saint-Honoré no. 283'. In Joséphine's bedroom, placed on an elegant mahogany table, there is a portable mirror also known as a *miroir à mettre sur ses genoux*, in the shape of a shield or heart supported by two finely moulded side pieces terminating in small Egyptian heads.

Later Biennais became official goldsmith to Napoleon, for whom he made a tea service, now in the Louvre, which is typical of the Empire style by reason of the inventive decoration and subtle modelling. He was a master who knew how to interpret the classical rules with originality and imagination, working in gold and tortoiseshell to create superlative snuff boxes, which the Emperor was fond of presenting to his generals and foreign diplomats visiting Paris. The architects Percier and Fontaine provided him with a collection of ornamental motifs appropriate to his artistic activity.

Empire clocks

During the Empire the art of metalwork found a multitude of uses in the production of artistic clocks of the pendulum type, which were real and accurate monuments in miniature. They were generally composed of groups or figures from mythology, almost always referring to the glorification of the Emperor, resting on bases of precious marble variously decorated or treated with an antique patina. They were usually placed on mantelpieces, *consoles* or desks.

At Malmaison there are many admirable clocks: 'Nymphs discovering Time', the work of the goldsmith Ravrio; the famous 'Chariot of Venus'; 'Jason winning the Golden Fleece'; and finally, the bronze gilt and marble clock presented at an exhibition sponsored by the Emperor which represents the First Consul crowned by the figure of Victory while Diogenes, who has finally found Man (Napoleon), extinguishes the lamp that had illuminated his search.

Snuff boxes

A brief mention must be made of the minute Empire snuff boxes, which, while lacking the refined grace of the perfume or patch boxes of the preceding century, had a certain style and richness of their own. Napoleon was fond of ordering every possible type to distribute generously on various occasions. He owned a vast collection for his personal use in gold or other precious metals, encrusted with gems, or in Sèvres porcelain decorated with splendid portrait miniatures of himself or his family. In a main clause of his will he wrote 'I leave to my son the snuff boxes'.

Finally, the flourishing factory of *papiers-peints* of the famous Réveillon, active under Louis XVI, was almost destroyed during the Revolution; what little remained was re-established by the partners Jacquemart and Bénard in 1791. They started to print wallpapers with the new symbolism of the revolutionaries: trees of liberty, red caps, cockades and so on. Then came the dazzling period of the *papier-peint*, portraying scenes alluding to events under Napoleon such as 'The French in Egypt', but the main production was dedicated to panoramic views, fantastic landscapes, and above all the coloured panels depicting curtains with the *trompe-l'oeil* (three dimensional) optical effect in soft tones.

Dufour in his Paris factory still produced compositions after David, while at Mulhouse Jean Zuber covered yards of paper with panoramic views framed by designs of curtains and decorative columns of classical style. From the decorator Laffitte came scenes after Prud'hon of which the best known is the 'Story of Psyche', while Fragonard the younger chose the delicious series with scenes from the 'Month of May'. The Empire style was to remain alive for many more years yet.

Bibliography

Charleston, R. J. (ed), *World Ceramics*, London 1968
Dauterman, C. C., *Sèvres*, London 1970
Dumonthier, Ernest, *Les Bronzes du Mobilier National: Bronzes d'Eclairage et de Chauffage*, Paris 1911
Dumonthier, Ernest, *Les Bronzes du Mobilier National: Pendules et Cartels*, Paris 1911
Dumonthier, Ernest, *Mobilier National de France: Les Sièges de Georges Jacob*, Paris 1921
Ernould-Gandouet, Marielle, *La Céramique en France au XIXᵉ siècle*, Paris 1969
Gonzalez-Palacios, Alvar, *The French Empire Style*, (translated from the Italian), London 1970
Grandjean, Serge, *Empire Furniture 1800–1825*, London 1966

Lafond, Paul, *L'Art décoratif et le Mobilier sous la République et l'Empire*, Paris 1900
Ledoux-Lebard, D., *Les Ebénistes Parisiens (1795–1830)*, Paris 1951
Lesur, A., and Tardy, *Les Porcelaines Françaises*, Paris 1967
Marie, Alfred, 'L'Album de Percier et Fontaine' in *Connaissance des Arts*, April, 1969
Masson, Frédéric, *Le Sacre et le Couronnement de Napoléon*, Paris 1908
Masson, Frédéric, *Napoléon chez lui: la Journée de l'Empereur aux Tuileries*, Paris 1894
Niclausse, Juliette, *Thomire*, Paris 1947
Taylor, Gerald, *Continental Gold and Silver*, London 1967

Index of artists

1 A corner of the Grand Salon at Malmaison, once used as a billiard room.

The salon is decorated with life-size portraits of Napoleon I and Joséphine Beauharnais in Imperial robes, by François Gérard (1770–1837). The room has recently been restored and the original furniture returned to it. A splendid pair of semicircular side-tables stand below the mirrors. The candle-branches of the wall-light are supported on a circular band of gilt bronze ornamented with laurel leaves (see detail, plate 82).

The great Savonnerie carpet displays the Napoleonic emblems: the large N at the centre, surrounded by bees, thunderbolts and Imperial stars. It was made to order for one of Napoleon's salons, and then given by Napoleon himself to the King of Saxony on 5 December 1809; returned to France after the Revolution, it is one of the few carpets that escaped destruction by succeeding dynasties.

Napoleon, First Consul for life, lived at Malmaison for a long period. The house offered hospitality to artists, writers and poets, who would help to design theatrical performances, banquets and festivals which both Napoleon and Joséphine enjoyed. After the divorce, Joséphine obtained from Napoleon the right to live at Malmaison, and she eventually died there on 29 May 1814.

In 1906 Malmaison became state property and was turned into a museum. Much of the original furnishing had disappeared or been relegated to the storehouses of the Mobilier National, where the best pieces were found, returned to the house, eventually to be set in their original positions.

2 Details of the semicircular side-table of carved and gilt wood.

The four legs are linked by very unusual stretchers. The pair to this side-table with a matching veined marble top upon which stands a dazzling Sèvres vase, is set against the opposite wall.

3   The music room, Malmaison.

This room was planned by Joséphine Bonaparte for Hortense, her daughter
by her first husband, the Vicomte Alexandre de Beauharnais. Hortense was
passionately fond of music and played both harp and piano extremely well.
Joséphine gave special thought to the furnishing of this room which led on
to a gallery (now destroyed) where the Empress's collection of paintings was
housed.

The arrangement of the furniture in this room accords with that shown in a
watercolour of 1812, painted by Auguste Garnerey. The two splendid mahogany
sofas and four armchairs bear the stamp of the Jacob brothers. The piano in the
centre of the room is an Erard of 1808; it was built for Queen Hortense of
Holland, stepdaughter of Napoleon. The twined legs terminate in sculptured
figures of winged sphinxes upon which the main body of the instrument rests.

The walls are hung with paintings by Girodet, Bergeret and Lemonnier,
works acquired by Joséphine and intended for her gallery.

The whole of Malmaison retains that atmosphere of intimacy which per-
meated the home that Joséphine acquired in April 1791. At that time Bonaparte
was in Egypt: on his return he was appointed First Consul, whereupon he
moved into Malmaison, entrusting the restoration and furnishing of his new
home to two young architects, Percier (1764–1838) and Fontaine (1762–1853).
The two artists transformed the old house, built on the site of a leper
colony belonging to the Abbey of Saint-Denis (hence the name Malmaison),
into a royal dwelling. In 1800 work on the rooms was finished. Joséphine then
turned her attention to the park and gardens, ordering several pavilions to be
built, as well as a Temple of Love, and a tiny theatre. Later she organized a
large heated greenhouse for tropical plants. During the Empire, Napoleon
left Malmaison for his other residences such as Saint-Cloud or Fontainebleau,
but Joséphine remained faithful to the old home she loved, never ceasing to
beautify and enlarge it.

G•IACOB JACOB·FRERES JACOB·D·
RUE MESLEE R·MESLEE

Harp. The music room, Malmaison.

This harp, which has a place of honour in the music room, is made of precious woods inlaid with mother-of-pearl and with gilt bronze mounts. It carries the signature of 'Cousieau father and son, Parisian lute-makers in the service of the Empress Joséphine'.

Joséphine herself, although lacking any particular aptitude for music, often liked to accompany her own singing. The lute-makers who signed the instrument took great care to make it worthy of its royal owner.

Fall-front *secrétaire*. Malmaison.

Veneered with mahogany and with ebony stringing and gilt bronze mounts, this *secrétaire* bears the stamp of Simon Mansion. The frieze is ornamented with gilt bronze festoons while the mounts on the vertical supports at each side include panoplies of arms of wholly classical derivation. Inside the fall-front is the dedicatory inscription: 'From your humble and obedient servant Mansion, in the year XIII'.

The stamps of the principal Empire furniture makers: Georges Jacob, the brothers Jacob and Jacob D. (Desmalter), the latter the most famous of all.

7 *Cabinet-commode*. Malmaison.

Also the work of Simon Mansion, this repeat[s] the decoration of festoons in gilt bronze and th[e] motif of multiple columns in miniature, all along th[e] front, resting on a high plinth. The piece is part o[f] the furnishings of the music room, and also bear[s] the cabinet-maker's dedicatory inscription.

A splendid clock rests on top of the piece, por[-]traying the 'Chariot of Venus', drawn by a swan. Th[e] marble base is decorated with cupids in variou[s] attitudes. The case is the work of the master Ravric[?] and is dated 1805.

8, 9 Small armchairs. Malmaison.

One piece is made of solid mahogany, with curv[-]ing backrest, upholstered in red woollen cloth.

The other armchair, with arm-rests, has delicat[e] bronze mounts. Both belong to the furnishing of th[e] music room at Malmaison and are the work of th[e] Jacob brothers.

7

8

9

10, 11   The council room, Malmaison.

This room was built in 1800 by the architects Percier and Fontaine at the express order of the First Consul, and was used as the grand council room. Designed to resemble a military tent with striped walls, it was restored during the Second Empire.

The decorative motifs underline the military aspect of the room. A dado of crossed lances runs along the walls; the door panels have war trophies in gilt bronze. In the centre of the room is a large mahogany table (reconstructed after a design by Percier and Fontaine). The armchairs and stools, with X-shaped supports, bear the stamp of the Jacob brothers. The bronze clock is composed of a bronze figure of Minerva and the clock face is the goddess's shield.

On the central table there is a *bouillotte* lamp with five arms branching from the base. The lampshade, in *tôle*, is adjustable and can be lowered to control the glare. This type of lamp, shown in the diagram, was already known in the preceding century, and called *bouillotte* because it was used to illuminate the table on which the card game *bouillotte* was played.

11

14

12 *Bouillotte* lamp. Malmaison.
This lamp is in gilt bronze with a green *tôle* lampshade with gilt decoration.

13 Wall-light. Malmaison.
This is one of the wall-lights in the council room. Each has five candle branches in gilt bronze supported on wings from which dart thunderbolts.

14 *Tabouret* or stool. Malmaison.
The stool is of ebonized wood, with legs of X-shape on lions' paw feet, and the details gilt. Both the stool and the chairs come from the council room of Saint Cloud and bear the sign of the Jacob brothers.

15

Andirons. Malmaison.

These fireplace decorations are made of gilt bronze in the form of a Roman met bound with laurel, resting on a base of metal with mouldings that eat the motif of wings and thunderbolts.

Salon known as 'Princesse Georges de Grèce', Malmaison.

Today this salon is also called the 'first exhibition room'. The major feature the decoration is the frieze which was originally in the green salon in the use in Rue de Chanteraine (later called the Rue de la Victoire), where neral Bonaparte and his wife Joséphine lived before 18 Brumaire (the day in 99 when Napoleon returned from Egypt). The decoration, saved when the house was demolished, was re-erected in a house in the Avenue d'Iéna in Paris and was recently given to Malmaison by the Princesse Georges de Grèce, née Marie Bonaparte.

The great Savonnerie carpet which covers the entire floor has a design of concentric circles, the outer circle enclosing pale blue sections with a design of swans back to back. In the centre there is a peacock. Set against the wall is a *bas-d'armoire* in mahogany, with two drawers and doors decorated in the centre with a gilt bronze wreath. Beside it are upholstered chairs. A mahogany pedestal supports a candelabrum with figures of winged sphinxes, and nearby this is a mahogany *jardinière* on two supports in the form of columns, with gilt details.

17 *Bas-d'armoire* veneered with mahogany. Malmaison.

The mahogany *bas-d'armoire* that occupies one wall of the salon has two doors decorated with large oak wreaths terminating in knotted ribbons. It belongs to the first years of the Empire period, and comes from the Tuileries; it bears the stamp of the cabinet-maker Marcion.

18 Pedestal. Malmaison.

The pedestal, which also forms part of the furnishings of the 'Princesse de Grèce' salon, is veneered with mahogany, exquisitely refined in line and workmanship; it is one of the vast array of *petits meubles* which serve as supports for candelabra, Sèvres vases or busts. The lower part is decorated with a subtle motif of a dancer framed in a diamond shape of gilt bronze, and this is surmounted by a frieze ornamented with two cornucopias. A similar motif is repeated on a *commode*, the work of Jacob Desmalter, housed in the Musée Marmottan in Paris.

19 Chair. Malmaison.

One of the chairs which make up part of the same furnishings at Malmaison, this piece is in the typically severe style of the Empire, and is upholstered in ivory-white satin, with bunches of brightly-coloured flowers in the centre of the seat and back-rest.

20   Dining room, Malmaison.

The dining room was originally enlarged at the Emperor's wish, who commissioned the Pompeian decorations. The walls are decorated with stucco panels painted with representations of dancing figures by the painter Laffitte.

The chairs, by the Jacob brothers, are extremely sober in design and quality, with their back-rests inlaid with ebony and brass. They come from the Library of the Elysée Palace, the dwelling assigned to Napoleon after his nomination as First Consul. On top of the sideboard are the two boat-shaped vessels made for the Emperor and Empress by the goldsmith Henri Auguste (1759–1816), both in silver-gilt adorned with splendid cast figures. These regal vessels, from medieval times traditionally offered to the sovereign by the city of Paris, were receptacles for the royal cutlery and table accessories to protect them from the dangers of poison.

On the table there are other pieces from the same service, which was presented to Napoleon on the occasion of his coronation, in 1803. The whole service comprised 590 pieces of which only 22 remain, Charles X having ordered the melting down of all the rest in his brief reign.

21   A dancer.

The figure is part of the group of panels painted by Laffitte for the decoration of the dining room at Malmaison.

20
21

22, 23 Bedroom of the Empress Joséphine, Malmaison.

The present furnishing has been reconstructed from the watercolour by Loeilliot who painted the Empress's room in 1810. On the walls and ceiling are beautiful deep red draperies embroidered in gold. The bed, the work of Jacob Desmalter, is of gilt wood with carved decoration. At the head are two swans, while the foot-rests are in the form of cornucopias. The curtains of white silk hang from a canopy in the form of a crown surmounted by an eagle. To the right of the bed is a mahogany dressing table on which is a *miroir de voyage* (portable mirror) in the form of a heart, bearing the stamp of Martin-Guillaume Biennais. The portable mirror could easily be dismantled and packed into the drawer that forms the base of this small piece of furniture.

Another Savonnerie carpet, with representations of swans, lyres and laurel branches, covers the whole floor. The gilt armchairs bear the initial of the Empress at the centre of the back-rest.

24 *Saut-de-lit* (wash-basin). Malmaison.

The tripod, in Joséphine's bedroom, is based upon Pompeian examples, and is dated about 1802. It supports a blue Sèvres porcelain wash-basin set in gilt bronze, borne by three winged sphinxes. In the centre of the tripod is a blue Sèvres porcelain ewer on a columnar support.

25 *Saut-de-lit*. Malmaison.

This is another wash-basin, a typical piece of Imperial furniture, in mahogany with gilt bronze mounts, from Joséphine's bathroom. The basin of Sèvres porcelain rests on four pillars surmounted by heads of naiads. The date of the piece is thought to be about 1805–6. It is the work of the cabinet-maker Marcion, but is not stamped.

26 Dressing-table. Malmaison.

This piece dominates Joséphine's bathroom. Veneered with burr elm and covered by a white marble top, it stands on X-shaped supports terminating in gilt bronze lions' paws. The oval mirror is flanked by two turned supports bearing candle branches. On the front of the drawers are gilt bronze ornaments.

27, 28 Octagonal table. Gold salon, Malmaison.

This magnificent salon contains an important octagonal *guéridon* table veneered with mahogany and with gilt bronze mounts attributed to Thomire. The slender gilt bronze columnar legs rest on a star-shaped mahogany base at the centre of which is a two-handled vase, also in gilt bronze.

The white marble fireplace, presented to Joséphine by Pope Pius VII, was originally decorated with precious stones and cameos, but these were destroyed during the occupation by the troops in 1870. The rich marble is decorated with symbols of the Empire.

Yellow salon, Fontainebleau.

This small suite belonging to the Empress was for some time used as a games room. It is one of the most beautiful in the palace, and is notable for the elegance of its furnishings.

The round, three-legged table, resting on a triangular base, has a sober decoration in gilt bronze. The floor is completely covered by a sumptuous Aubusson carpet with a white background. A *bouillotte* lamp with green lampshade stands in the centre of the table. The splendid side-table is decorated with fine bas-relief by Thomire, representing the triumph of Trajan. On the table are two candelabra, also made by Thomire, portraying winged victories on high bronze bases. The entire salon retains the original character visualized by Napoleon in 1809, when he commissioned the Jacob brothers to furnish it. The old gold upholstery of the chairs and armchairs is in *gros de Naples* with embroidery in amaranth silk. The wall panels and fire-screen are of the same material.

30

30 Yellow room, Malmaison.

This room is known as the Emperor's bedroom, although there is no proof that Napoleon actually slept here. The only certainty is that during his first years at Malmaison, the First Consul had a bedroom furnished for him adjoining Joséphine's boudoir; later, another room was prepared for him which might have been this one.

The decor is pure Empire in its severe simplicity. Everything in the room indicates a later redecoration in keeping with the style of the epoch, and recalls Napoleon's signed instructions on a complicated interior decoration plan: 'Simplify more: it is for the Emperor'.

Heavy ivory silk curtaining covers the walls of this room, which contains a simple mahogany bed with sparse decorations in gilt bronze. A small *guéridon* table, with a bold central support and three column-shaped legs, rests on a triangular base. Armchairs and chairs upholstered in yellow silk with brown ribbon embroidery complete the furnishings. On the table is a *bouillotte* lamp.

31 *Saut-de-lit*. The Emperor's bedroom, Fontainebleau.

This mahogany wash-basin has three legs and a basin supported by swans. In the centre is a triangular shelf decorated by three finely finished dolphins.

32 The Emperor's bedroom. The *Grands Appartements*, Fontainebleau.

The furnishing of this room was supervised by Jacob. Bed, chairs, armchairs and fire-screen are covered in a fine velvet *à ramages* (floral pattern) from the factories of Lyons. Near the bed is a mahogany bedside cupboard with a graceful decoration around the top and an amphora motif on the door. On both sides of the sumptuous bed canopy are two Roman helmets bound with laurel wreaths.

31

33 Napoleon's study, Fontainebleau.

When Napoleon first moved into Fontainebleau, he occupied the mezzanine floor; these rooms were called the *Petits Appartements*. In 1810 he moved to the first floor, where he had a new bedroom and study, containing this superb mahogany desk with its refined decoration in front: bees, seahorses and stylized leaves. The desk top rests on four heavy lions' paws interconnected by a broad stretcher.

34 *Bonheur-du-jour*. Musée des Arts Décoratifs, Paris.

In figured mahogany, this small piece is dated between 1805 and 1810 and bears the stamp of the cabinet-maker Charles Joseph Lemarchand (1759–1826). It has two doors, decorated with mythological figures in gilt bronze, and belongs to the category of *petits meubles* dear to the ladies of the epoch. The drawer of the base is decorated with two winged figures flanked by lions, a motif recalling that on the side-table at Malmaison.

35 *Commode* in plum-pudding mahogany. Fontainebleau.

In both structure and decoration, this piece is an admirable example of good proportion and simplicity. It has three drawers framed between two uprights terminating above in bronze capitals and below in lions' paws. Light motifs in the form of stars and crowns enliven the handles of the drawers, while the keyholes are decorated with seahorses. The top of the chest of drawers is in precious turquoise marble. The date of the work is 1809–10.

36

37

34

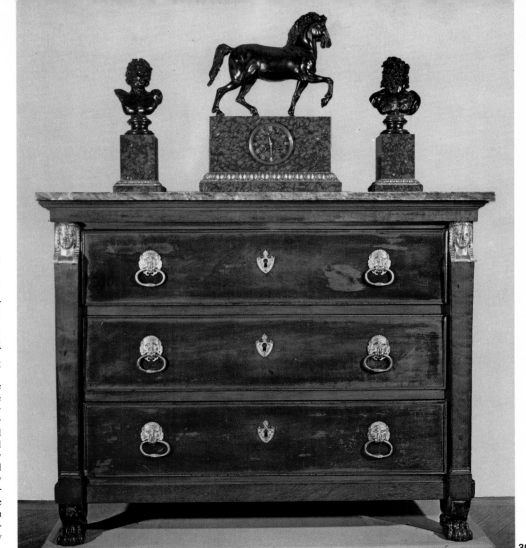

and 39 Two chests of drawers (1809–10).
The first of these two pieces is veneered with flame [ma]hogany, the second in plain mahogany but they [ea]ch have marble tops, and their general shape and [de]coration is the same. The vertical supports each [sid]e are surmounted by gilt bronze masks of [Eg]yptian character, with feet in the form of lions' [pa]ws. One has four and the other three drawers and [the]ir keyholes are decorated with shields, palm [lea]ves and stylized designs of leaves. The handles of [th]e drawers are composed of lions' masks holding [rin]gs.

The Empire *commodes* or chests of drawers and the [corp]s-d'armoire with three or at most four drawers, are [ge]nerally rectangular, resting on plinths, or they may [ha]ve no feet, and sit directly on the floor. They [be]long to the category of large furniture, and [oc]cupy a position of great importance in the royal [su]ites. Their severity of line is often compensated by [th]e wood used – generally mahogany, much prized [fo]r its durability and the magnificent polish that may [be] obtained – was imported from America. After [th]e Continental Blockade, which prevented the [im]portation of any foreign merchandise, Napoleon [en]couraged the use of French woods. The cabinet-[m]akers were forced to fall back on mahogany [su]bstitutes such as elm root, ash, beech and yew.

39

40

38

[37] Mahogany *guéridon* table. Musée des Arts [Dé]coratifs, Paris.
This table, which dates back to the first years of [th]e Empire, could be adapted to various uses, its [sid]e handles facilitating easy transport from one [ro]om to another. The simplicity of decoration and [th]e sobriety of structural line are characteristic. [A] top drawer and small storage space behind two [do]ors served to contain sewing, embroidery or even [wr]iting materials.

[38] Palm leaves, acanthus leaves and rosettes [co]nstitute part of the rich decorative repertoire [ad]opted by furniture-makers, bronze-smiths, and [ot]her workers of the Empire period, and all these [en]riched the front and sides of furniture.

[39] Semicircular side-table. Reception salon, [M]almaison.
This large mahogany side-table is the work of [Ja]cob Desmalter. Two splendid chimeras in green [pa]tinated bronze support the white marble top [de]corated with a precious mosaic of coloured [m]arbles. The two chimeras rest on a high mahogany [ba]se. The semicircular front strip displays a design [of] palm leaves, and the piece is backed by a mirror.

41 *Secrétaire en abattant*. Fontainebleau.

This *secrétaire* is veneered with mahogany. Strictly geometric in shape, it framed by two vertical supports surmounted by Egyptian heads. The top draw is separated from the three lower ones by a fall-front. The keyholes are adorn with the usual motifs of stylized palms, while the handles and their rings a formed by lions' heads in gilt bronze. Dating back to 1805, this piece is faith to the designs of the architects Percier and Fontaine, which were carried out the cabinet-makers who worked under their direction.

42 *Commode* in plum-pudding mahogany. Musée des Arts Décoratifs, Paris.

This is a classic piece of the Empire period, dating from between 1805— The work bears the stamp of C. Lemarchand. The bronze mounts of the cent part, representing a mythological scene, are particularly well modelled, as a the two winged dancers at the sides. Two caryatids with Egyptian heads s mount the trusses and the top drawer is further enriched by two laurel wreat There is an elaborate pierced floral design in gilt bronze around the keyhole.

41

42

43 44

Mahogany *secrétaire*. Fontainebleau.
Designed by the architects Percier and Fontaine, this was the work of the cabinet-maker Bennemann, a ʃster who had been much appreciated and extremely active at the court of Louis XVI. The piece marks the ɲnsition between the neoclassical and Empire styles. The fall-front is decorated with unusual figures of erub musicians in gilt bronze, while the recumbent figures of two facing lions, reminiscent of fire-dogs, corate the lower half. At the corners, trusses surmounted by stylized sphinxes rest on columns.

Night table (*somno*). Fontainebleau.
The name *somno* is given to bedside night tables of the Empire. The table usually had one highly decorated or, and one small drawer. Almost all the Empire style beds, from the *lit en bateau* to the straight-backed re accompanied by a night table, often with decoration repeating the principal motifs of the bed coration.
This example is part of the furnishing of the rooms occupied by Pius VII. The elegant decoration consists of ow of stars above, and a stylized wreath on the door surrounding a medallion of blue enamel. This piece d the bed that accompanies it (see 79) are not attributed to any particular master.

45

46

47

48

45 *Commode à vantaux*

This *commode* is of the type adopted by the Jacob brothers. It is decorated with the usual laurel wreaths and antique vases. The central door encloses a tier of drawers.

46 Mahogany desk. Malmaison.

This desk is probably the work of Charles Lemarchand. Its bronze mounts are reminiscent of those on the small *bonheur-du-jour* in the Musée des Arts Décoratifs, in Paris.

On the top of the desk is a small chest of drawers, the ends of which are supported by caryatids.

47 *Commode* in mahogany and satinwood. Fontainebleau.

The central panel is inlaid with a robed figure, framed by a motif of ivy vines and flowers, the same motif of ivy that decorates the two side panels. All the inlays are in polychrome woods, tin and ivory. The piece bears the stamp of the brothers Jacob, and was made in 1800-2.

48 Dressing-table in yew root. Musée des Arts Décoratifs, Paris.

This piece almost certainly belonged to the Empress Joséphine's boudoir at the Tuileries, and differs from that of Malmaison in the octagonal shape of the mirror, the sobriety of its decoration, and the four legs in the form of lyres. It bears the date 1805 and the stamp of Jacob Desmalter.

50

52

51

49,50   The throne of Napoleon 1. Musée des Arts Décoratifs, Paris.

Designed by the architects Charles Percier (1764–1838) and Pierre François Fontaine (1762–1853), this throne was destined for the Council of Deputies. It is of massive design and decoration, weighted down by gilding and by the various emblems – the winged lions, the crossed sceptres of the back-rest, and the laurel wreath – and it is completed by an enormous velvet cushion. The back is surmounted by a large Imperial crown. On a *lunette* below there was originally the Napoleonic N enclosed by a laurel wreath held by ribbons. This was hastily removed at the fall of the Empire.

51   Work Table.

It has a sober decoration on the front apron: the legs are formed as paired columns with gilt bronze ornamentation. A silk bag is intended to hold balls of wool and handiwork.

52   *Guéridon en athénienne*. Fontainebleau.

The *guéridon*, already popular in the preceding century, takes on a new style during the Empire period, known as *en athénienne*, with obvious classical references. It comprises a central support, sometimes of crossed iron or bronze straps, on which the mahogany or metal top rests. The date of the piece is about 1804–5.

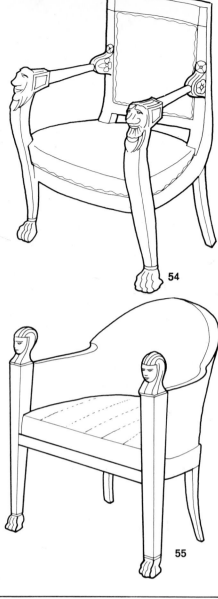

54

55

53

53 *Athénienne.*

Athéniennes had various uses and were placed both reception and private suites.

This example is in mahogany with a circul marble top, encircled by a finely chased gilt bron mount. The three legs, with gilt bronze termina rest on a triangular base. In the centre of this the is a circular pedestal on which a jug or oth ornament could be placed. The piece is distinguishe in its elegance of line and still more in the sobrie of its decoration. It may have been accompanied l a jug and basin in Sèvres porcelain, and could ha been used as a *saut-de-lit* or wash-basin in son room at court.

54, 55 The principal characteristics of armchai in Empire style are the rigid back and rectiline arms. Ornamentation is applied to the intersectio of the front legs; other features are the claw feet ar the motifs of sphinxes, lion masks or small Egyptia heads on the arms. Typical armchairs have arn carved in the form of fully modelled swans such those executed by Desmalter for the Empress Jos phine at Malmaison.

56 Mahogany *guéridon*. Musée des Arts Décor tifs, Paris.

This is another type of *guéridon* in mahogan probably dating back to the years of the Consula (1799–1804). The central pedestal with gilt orname on a painted bronze ground rests on a triangula mahogany base.

57   Reception armchair.

A piece such as this, an apparent anachronism among the rigid Empire arm-chairs, takes us back to the Louis XVI period, with its broad oval back in one piece, and short, padded armrests. The splendid material from the *Manufacture* of Lyons is woven with a typical motif of baskets of flowers.

58   Armchair in painted and gilt wood. Malmaison.

This elegant and spectacular armchair was one of several that made their first appearance at Saint-Cloud, where they were destined for the private suite of Joséphine. She had them moved to Malmaison, where they have remained.

Every detail has a refined elegance and creates an overall impression of striking romanticism. This model, called *en gondole*, was made by Jacob Desmalter to designs of the architect Percier. The Empress's favourite swan motif predominates in the wood sculpture and in the design of the upholstery. The two swans that terminate the arms bear a golden necklace around their necks. The cover, in white *gros de Tours*, is patterned with golden stars and a central medallion of two swans back to back. The same motif is repeated on the seat cushion.

An identical motif of addorsed swans is repeated on the firescreen (see 90); the predominating motif however is the Napoleonic letter N surrounded by a laurel wreath, particularly in fabrics for wall panels or curtaining.

59   Mahogany *guéridon*. Malmaison.

The three sabre legs support the top of the table, and below this is a circular mahogany frieze decorated with stylized palm leaves. A gilt bronze gallery completes the ornamentation.

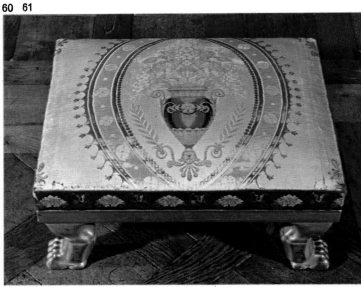

60 61

62

60, 61, 62 Chair, foot-stool and *canapé causeus[e]*. Fontainebleau.

The small *causeuse* is in carved wood, with th[e] back-rest curved at the top; the back legs are sab[re] shaped, while the front legs, in the form [of] Egyptian caryatids, terminate in lions' paws. Th[e] cover is of silk, woven with motifs of medallio[ns] and stylized vases of flowers, and along the fro[nt] there is an alternating design of palm leaves an[d] stylized acanthus. The fabric comes from the Lyo[ns] silk factories, which owed their rebirth to th[e] encouragement of the Emperor. For establishing [a] new court protocol that obliged courtiers [to] refurnish their houses in a sumptuous and extrava[-] gant manner, Napoleon hoped to encourag[e] national industry and provide employment for th[e] workmen, who would be required to produc[e] materials and designs corresponding to the ne[w] tastes. Thus the production of the various fabri[cs] flourished: splendid damasks, velvets, and taffet[as] (*gros de Tours* and *gros de Naples*) in soft past[el] tones inspired by the designs of famous artists.

The chair matches the *causeuse*, differing only i[n] the front legs, which are turned and carved; the bac[k] legs are sabre shaped.

The footstool that completes the trio displays th[e] central motif of the design and rests on lions' paw[s] which echo those of the *causeuse*. The stamp is tha[t] of Jacob Desmalter and the piece is dated arour[d] 1803–5.

3 Small table in elm root. Fontainebleau.
The top of this table lifts up to reveal a mirror and writing surface. It has
partly gilt, partly patinated X-shaped legs linked by a slender column. It is
attributed to Thomire, about 1805.

4 Armchair and footstool in gilt wood and velvet. Fontainebleau.
The armchair is very handsome, upholstered in figured golden green velvet
from the *Manufacture* at Lyons. It is part of a splendid set comprising a *divan-
useuse*, similar to the *méridienne* in style because of its irregular back, a screen,
the little footstool, and a firescreen. The set was designed by P. G. Brion, on the
orders of Napoleon, for the furnishing of the second salon in the *Petits Appartements* of the mezzanine floor at Fontainebleau.

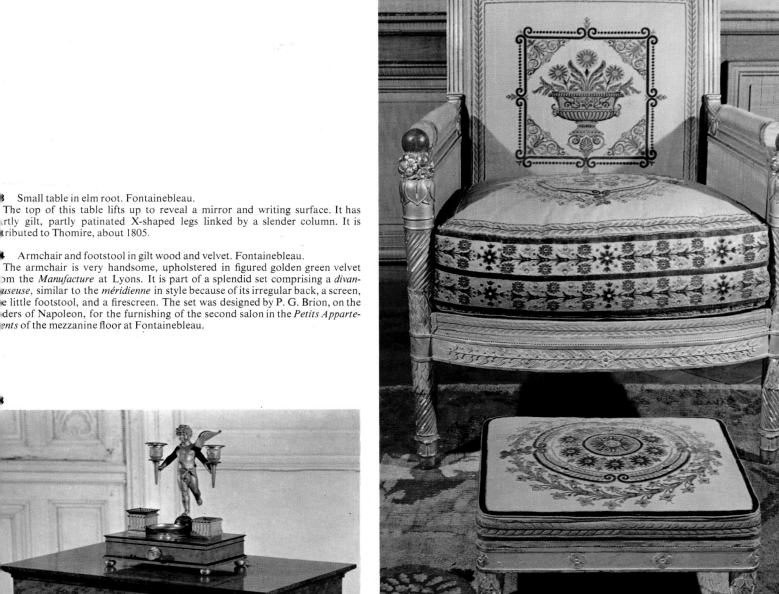

64

65 Mahogany armchair. Musée des Arts Décoratifs, Paris.

This piece is in the shape of a curule (or camp-stool). The armchair rests on X-shaped front legs, while the back legs are sabre shaped. The open-work back has a central motif of a tripod, and the seat is in green velvet; dated about 1800.

66 *Causeuse* in carved gilt wood. Fontainebleau.

The Empress Joséphine's room in the *Petits Appartements* at Fontainebleau was designed in 1808 by the Jacob brothers. The furnishing consists of a large bed, accompanied by the *causeuse* with its footstool and a series of armchairs. The curtains that adorn the monumental bed are of the same brocade as the wall panels, woven with rosette motifs, and finished in a beautiful pastel tint. The armchairs and *causeuse* have a straight back typical of the Napoleonic epoch, decorated with delicate running-scroll carvings, and the padded arm-rests terminate in carved decoration. The ornate mirror frame over the fireplace, the work of Biennais, is also an important feature of the room. Next to the Empress's room is the bathroom, where there is a bath cunningly disguised as a padded divan, designed by the Emperor himself and made by Jacob.

65
66

67 Mahogany chair. Malmaison.
One of the remarkable chairs housed at Malmaison, this is in full Empire style, and made by the Jacob brothers in partly gilded mahogany, with an upholstered seat. The back curves over at the top and is decorated with palm leaf motifs; the central design is of formal open-work leaves. The back legs are sabre shaped, while the front ones terminate in lions' paws of gilt bronze and the point of junction with the seat is masked by gilt bronze mounts. This chair originally came from the Tuileries.

68 Armchair of mahogany. Musée des Arts Décoratifs, Paris.
This elegant chair with its curving back dates from about 1800; the high back-rest is decorated by a laurel wreath and a spiral design of inlaid ebony. The front legs are turned columns and the back is sabre shaped. The high arm-rests are padded in blue, like the seat, and terminate in carved lions' heads.

69

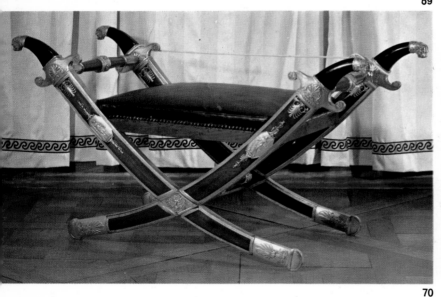

70   71

69   Napoleon's paper holder. Malmaison.

This small piece is in the form of a shield, and is kept in Napoleon's library where it was used to hold his papers and journals. Executed in solid mahogany with gilt bronze mounts of fine workmanship, it bears the mark of the maker Biennais.

70   *Tabouret* seat. Malmaison.

This is a typical Empire stood with crossed sabre shaped legs, richly finished with gilded bronze motifs. The seat is upholstered in velvet.

71   Large rectangular *psyché* mirror in mahogany. Fontainebleau.

The mirror forms part of the furnishings of the apartment of Maria Letizia Bonaparte, the Emperor's mother. The frame and stand are decorated with rosette motifs; in the centre of the pediment is the ritual laurel wreath.

72   The fireplace of the 'Abdication' salon. Fontainebleau.

The rich decoration on three sides, with bronze motifs, is complemented two splendid fire-dogs of massive gilt bronze, in the shape of classical fune urns.

73   Fireplace in red marble. Fontainebleau.

Extremely simple in line, the fireplace is enriched by two fire-dogs of bronze, finely modelled with classical votive lamps on which are seated winged female figures. This fireplace is in the yellow drawing-room of Empress's *Petits Appartements*.

74
75

74 Fireplace in red marble. Versailles.

This admirable work of the Rousseau brothers belongs to the last years of the Louis XVI style, but resembles the Empire style in its ornamentation and line. It has motifs of circles and rosettes in gilt bronze, while the *consoles* at each end terminate in female heads.

75 Hearth ornament in gilt bronze with antique patina. Malmaison.

On the front of the base is a classical scene with seated figures warming themselves before the flames of a votive altar; on the two side panels are subjects symbolizing music. A black bronze animal crouches on the top in front of a vase filled with flowers.

76 Mahogany bed. Musée des Arts Décoratifs, Paris.

This bed has two curved ends, and is decorated at the corners with carved swans painted in imitation of antique bronze. The frieze is embellished with gilt bronze figures of cupids riding seahorses, and at the two ends are laurel wreaths enclosing the heads of classical figures. The solid legs are square.

77 Mahogany bed. Musée des Arts Décoratifs, Paris.

This type is known as the *en bateau*, and is ornamented in front by classical female figures. Two sphinxes are carved at the tops of the vertical panels at each end.

78
79

52

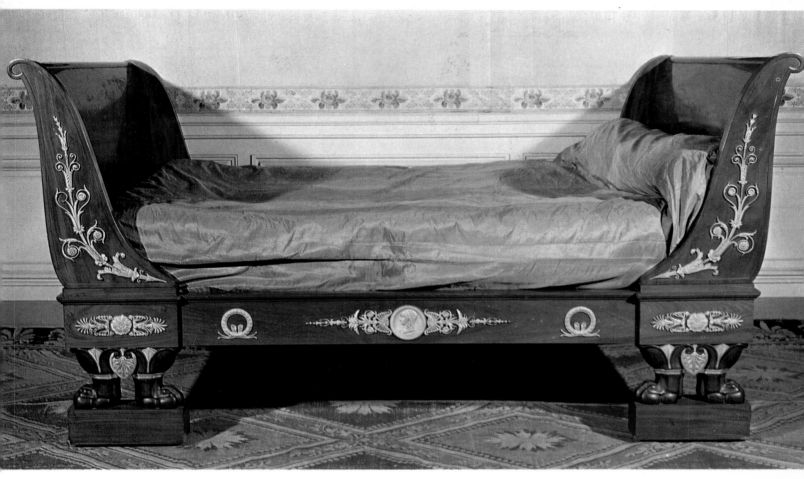

81

Mahogany and bronze bed. Fontainebleau.
In this piece, the two bed heads or ends are straight: the rear ends are higher, ʳminating in a small urn, while the front ends are supported by a base and ʳminate in a modelled Greek head, above which rises a classical vase. Dated ᵗween 1810–15.

Bed with curved ends. Fontainebleau.
This is in mahogany decorated with medallions in blue enamel, linked by a gilt ᵒnze ornament. The bed, with its bedside cupboard (see 44), belonged to the ᵈroom occupied by Pius VII at Fontainebleau. Although obviously the work ᵃ good craftsman, it has no identifying mark.

Mahogany bed en bateau.
This bed, with curved ends, is ornamented with superb mounts of flowering ᵃnches and medallions in gilt bronze.

Applique (wall bracket) in carved and gilt wood. Malmaison.
In the form of a swan with spread wings, splendidly carved, the appliques of ˢéphine's bathroom bear the gilded bronze candle-holders on their heads and ᵗstretched wings.

82 Bronze *applique*.
In this case, the candle branches are inserted in a finely chased gilt bro[n]
crown, by the goldsmith to the Court, Pierre Philippe Thomire.

83 Bronze candelabrum. Musée des Arts Décoratifs, Paris.
This is one of the two candelabra that decorate each side of the bed (see 7[
A bronze sphinx rises from a base decorated with chimeras and cupids in relief

84 Bronze lamp. Malmaison.
Resting on a tripod of graceful and elegant lines are three winged cupids
patinated bronze, holding the chased gilt bronze vase that supports [
candlesticks.

85 Lamp *en girandole*. Malmaison.
This piece is composed of a winged victory holding aloft a laurel cro[
on which are the candle holders. The rare talents of the metalsmith Thomire [
revealed in the chromatic effect obtained by the contrast between gilt bro[n]
and bronze with antique patina.

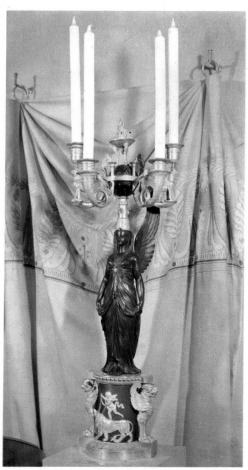

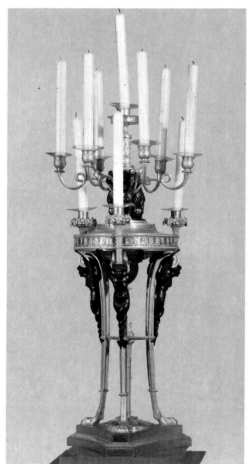

82

83   84

86

87

86 Oil lamp. Musée des Arts Décoratifs, Paris.

This lamp is also known as the 'Quinquet', after its inventor. Although of common material – lacquered tin and painted bronze – this lamp conserves a certain classical quality clearly shown in the Roman head with plumed helmet and the decorations of the main support.

87 Diogenes clock. Malmaison.

The theme of this monumental clock is the First Consul being crowned by Victory while Diogenes extinguishes his lantern, having at last found the Man (Napoleon). The splendid dark green marble base is adorned with symbols and figures dear to Napoleon.

88 'The Nymph discovering Time'. Malmaison.

Gilt bronze and bronze with antique patina are juxtaposed in this superb representation of the Nymph discovering Time. The marble base is enriched with applications of gilt bronze and figures drawn from the classical repertoire.

88

89

89 'The Chariot of Minerva'. Malmaison.

This superb clock in gilt and antique bronze represents the Chariot of Minerva drawn by two finely modelled racing horses. The dial of the clock is inserted in the chariot wheel. The high black marble base, enclosed at the four corners by the *fasces*, Roman symbol of judicial authority, displays the usual laurel wreaths and an eagle with outspread wings.

90 Firescreen. Malmaison.

The motif of swans back to back, dear to the Empress Joséphine, is repeated in this elegant firescreen of silk from Lyons, enriched by decorations of garlands in soft colours. The side supports and frame are in mahogany and the legs have lions' paws.

91 Large vase in Sèvres porcelain. Malmaison.

This large 'crater' vase is made of hard Sèvres porcelain. On one side is a painted view of the Château de Sans-Souci, at Potsdam. Brilliant colours and precious gilding ornament this excellent piece, which dates from about 1805.

92, 93, 94, 95 Four splendid plates in Sèvres porcelain. Malmaison.

Plates, dishes, utensils and vases became much simpler in shape under the Empire; cups took on more angular lines, losing their former grace, while jugs were transformed into amphoras and classical 'crater' vases or cups, and sugar bowls became miniature tripods. The decoration followed the official rule book, the plates depicting views, recent historical events, or portraits of the Emperor, Joséphine and Marie-Louise. Stars, bees, and Roman swords decorated the wide rims of plates, the rims of sugar bowls and the great amphoras. Napoleon also ordered from Sèvres services of plates showing the Imperial residences. The remaining pieces of the table service that Napoleon wished to take into exile to Saint Helena are at Malmaison. One of these plates has a view of the waterfalls of Saint-Cloud, another has a view of Malmaison, while on another the ostrich in an oriental landscape records Napoleon's campaign in Egypt. The rims are decorated with alternation motifs of stars and swords in gold on a background of Corsican green, with facing swans, interwoven medallions, ribbons and floral garlands.

96

97

98

96   Cup and saucer. Malmaison.
On the cup and the rim of the saucer there is a design of birds drinking from a vase, purely Pompeian in stylistic inspiration. The whole inside of the cup is gilded. These two pieces come from the factory of Honoré Dagety, which under Joséphine's patronage, was granted the title *Manufacture de l'Impératrice*.

97   Large cup with saucer in the form of a swan. Malmaison.
On the dark saucer, decorated with a white motif in relief, the hard paste cup stands in the form of a white swan with its bent neck forming the handle. The inside of the cup, which could also be used as a sauceboat, is gilded all over.

98   Cup with two handles in hard paste porcelain. Malmaison.
The whole inside is gilded; the handles are formed as reversed cornucopias full of flowers, and the cameo ornament is surrounded by a decoration of small stars.

99   Drawing of an opaline vase.
Opaline was made in the eighteenth century from coloured or milk-white glass. During the Empire its value increased, as it was made from pure transparent crystal. The shapes are classical in design, and the material offers the possibility of unusual reflections: orange, rose, yellow or the splendour of the iridescent lilac known as 'pigeon's throat'.

102

100 Glass-holder. Musée des Arts Décoratifs, Paris.
This work in silvered bronze by the goldsmith Claude Odiot (1763–1850) belongs to a great service executed by the artist with the new technique of cold mounting. It takes the form of two glass-holders shaped like crowns, held up by three cherubs with wings. At the centre is a small column surmounted by a female figure with large wings and outstretched arms holding two garlands.

101 Silver soup-tureen. Malmaison.
This tureen is part of the service presented to Napoleon on his coronation by the city of Paris. Made by Henri Auguste (1759–1816), the service consisted of more than five hundred pieces, of which only 22 are left. A finely chased border follows the rim of the bowl and pedestal, which is enriched by winged sphinxes with lions' paws alternating with the Imperial coats-of-arms.

102 Sauceboat. Musée des Arts Décoratifs, Paris.
The sauceboat is the work of Claude Odiot (1763–1850). A graceful young satyr holds up a small bath which has a butterfly with closed wings as a handle. The heavy pedestal is enlivened by a group of modelled cherubs.
Odiot had a preference for naturalistic subjects. His works were for the most part inspired by the designs of the architects Percier and Fontaine, as well as those of the goldsmith Henri Auguste, from whom he obtained models and designs when the latter went bankrupt – an acquisition which allowed him to complete the service commissioned for the coronation of Napoleon.

103 Inkwell in porcelain and biscuit. Malmaison.
Precious because of its imaginative quality and execution, the inkwell com[es]
from the porcelain factory of Dagoty. The winged cherub is in biscuit, as a[re]
the decorations on the base, while the rest is in hard porcelain. This is [a]
remarkable example of the high quality work produced by the French porcela[in]
manufacturers of the day, one of the best being the factory of Dago[ty]
favourite supplier to the Empress, and second in importance only to Sèvres. T[he]
date is about 1805.

104 Wall hanging. Malmaison.
This material came from the silk factories at Lyons. It is a blue brocade with[a]
lyre motif among garlands and leaves interspersed with stars.

103
104

105

105 Wall hanging. Malmaison.

This fragment of brocade, made in 1804 by the Pernon factory of Lyons for Joséphine's salon at Saint-Cloud, is in gold and silver on an azure damask background. The centre of the material features myrtle and ivy wreaths alternating with palm leaves, roses, and silver stars. The wide border has garlands of marguerites in silver and gold.

The fabrics of Camille Pernon were among the first to make use of the technical innovations introduced by Joseph-Marie Jacquard (1752–1834) whose mechanical looms were shown for the first time at the industrial Exhibition of Paris in 1801. The looms increased the rate of production without any loss of quality, and it became necessary to provide an even wider range of fabrics and designs to satisfy consumer demand, expanded as a result of the Napoleonic policy of court protocol which obliged nobles and courtiers to refurnish their houses in the sumptuous new style.

106 Fragment of tapestry. Malmaison.

The motif of the two swans stands out against a background enclosed in a golden circle, while a second circle of olive leaves and palm surrounds a pale yellow zone. At the bottom is a festoon of gaily coloured flowers bound by red ribbons.

This fabric comes from Pernon of Lyons and was originally created for Joséphine's salon at Saint-Cloud. Later, in 1812, it was taken to Malmaison (see 90).

106

107
108

107 Design by Huet for a printed fabric. Malmaison.

This is a typical example of the type of decoration of canvases and linens of Jouy, used in upholstery. The models are evidently drawn from classical antiquity.

108 Chair back. Malmaison.

The chair back illustrated is in *gros de Tours*, with bright flowers and leaves on a white background *semé* with green crosses. Made about 1803, the chair's fabric came from the Pernon factory at Lyons. It was in Joséphine's small drawing room at Saint-Cloud, until taken to Malmaison in 1812.

109 Design of *papier-peint*. Malmaison.

This wallpaper design simulates curtaining, and is enriched at the top with folds and with bunches of flowers. At the bottom are small framed landscapes.

110 Fragment of material. Malmaison.

Made by the Pernon factory at Lyons, this material – brocade with stylized leaves, flowers and gold rosettes on a white background – was part of the furnishings for Joséphine's drawing-room at Saint-Cloud. It was taken to Malmaison in 1812.

111 Detail of a Savonnerie carpet. Malmaison.

This enormous carpet is one of the most beautiful known, despite its bad state of repair, and is still a part of the furnishing in the 'Princesse Georges de Grèce' room. The design of concentric circles is divided into sections enclosing swans set back to back. Bands of lance-shaped leaves alternate with floral stripes.

The crisis in the Savonnerie carpet factory that resulted from the Revolution, was solved by Napoleon and the new aristocracy by the continuous and numerous orders placed by them for the refurnishing of Imperial and private residences. Among the many designers working at Savonnerie, the decorator La Hamayade de Saint-Ange, who was appointed designer to the Mobilier Impérial in 1802, was the most important. His designs were undoubtedly the best used by the carpet manufactory.

112 Detail of carpet. Malmaison.

This is part of the furnishing of Empress Joséphine's bedroom. The central motif repeats the symbol of the swan, a blue background contrasting with the bright red of the other surrounding symbols.

112